SAVING THE BALD EAGLES

MW00908411

by Kathy Furgang

Table of Contents

Where Can You Find Bald Eagles?

Bald eagles are beautiful birds that live only in North America. Most live in Canada or Alaska.

The bald eagle is the national bird of the United States. It is a symbol of freedom to the American people.

ALASKA
(U.S.A.)

C A N A D A

U N I T E D

S T A T E S

Bald eagles are among the biggest birds in North America. When they fly, their wings span more than seven feet.

wingspan

Bald eagles have great eyesight.
This helps them find food.
They eat fish, rabbits, turtles, and other
small animals. They catch food
in their strong beaks and sharp claws.

Why Were Bald Eagles in Danger?

Bald eagles were in danger for many years. Many bald eagles were killed by hunters.

Many bald eagles lost their homes when people cut down trees to make land for new towns.

Many bald eagles died from a spray that people used to kill bugs.
Bald eagles needed help.

A spray called DDT was used from the 1940s to the 1970s. This spray made bald eagles' eggs very weak. The eggs were so weak that not many hatched.

In the 1960s, scientists said bald eagles were endangered. There would be no more bald eagles if people did not make a change.

How Did People Help Bald Eagles?

Many people wanted to help the bald eagles. They made new laws to protect bald eagles.

They made a law to stop people
from cutting down trees with eagle nests.
They made a law to stop people
from hunting bald eagles. They made
a law to stop people from using
the spray that harmed eagles.

People also helped bald eagles
that were sick or hurt. The birds
were given food and care.

When the eagles were well again,
they were let go to live on their own.

How Are Bald Eagles Doing Today?

People worked for years
to save bald eagles.
Their work paid off!

Bald eagles are no longer endangered.
Today, thousands of them live
in North America. People still watch them
to make sure they stay safe.

People learned that we can do things
to hurt animals. They also learned that
we can do things to help animals.
They learned that we must make
the world safe for living things.